Comprehension Boo

C000230571

CONTENTS

Walpole

Way up north where it is always cold, there lived a great herd of walruses. The biggest was Walpole. Walpole loved the cold.

Sometimes the walruses pushed each other to get the best place on the rocks. But they never tried to push Walpole.

"It's time for you to lead the herd," said the oldest walrus. "You are the biggest and the strongest. Polar bears never come near us when they see your tusks."

"I don't want to be a leader," said Walpole. "I want to take care of baby walruses who have lost their mothers."

Walpole gave the little walruses rides on his back as if he were their mother. He found food for them on the ocean floor. And he made sure they did not float away on a piece of ice.

The little walruses loved Walpole. They barked like puppy dogs when he walked on his flippers and shook all over.

"Please be our leader," said the oldest walrus again.

"No," said Walpole. "I'm having too much fun."

Syd Holt from *Walpole* (World's Work Children's Book)

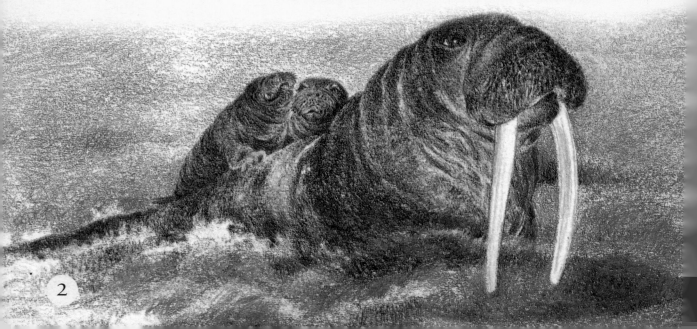

1   Why did the oldest walrus want Walpole to be the leader?

     He wanted Walpole to be the leader because Walpole was the
     _____ and the _____ walrus in the herd.

2   What did Walpole want to do instead of being the leader?

     Walpole wanted to look after _____ who had lost
     their _____ .

3   What did the baby walruses love to see Walpole doing?

     They loved to see him walk on his _____ and
     _____ all over.

4   What kind of things did Walpole do for the little walruses?

     He gave them _____ on his back.
     He found _____ for them.
     He made sure that they didn't _____ away on a piece
     of _____ .

5   What animals would never hurt the walruses if Walpole was there?

     The _____ would never hurt the walruses if Walpole
     was there.

Making a moving cat

You will need:
card
pencil
paper fasteners
scissors
paints

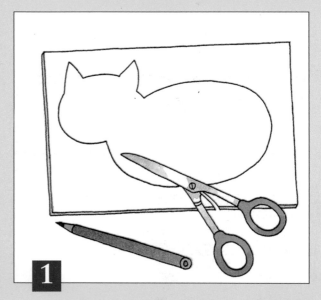

1

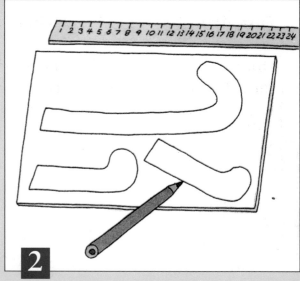

2

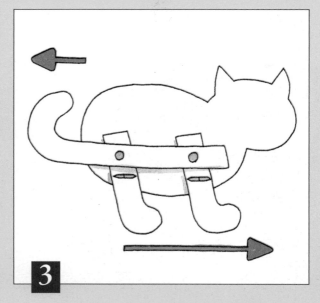

3

4

Write out the instructions in the correct order to explain how to make a moving cat. Use the pictures to help you. *(3 marks each for correct order + 3 marks for spelling, punctuation and handwriting)*

Finally, paint the cat's face and body on the other side of the card.

Fix the legs only to the back of the cat's body with paper fasteners. Fix the tail to the top of the legs, but not to the body, with fasteners. Now you can move the tail and the legs will also move.

First, draw the shape of a cat's head and body on card and cut it out.

Draw two legs and a tail, making sure they are at least 2 cm wide. The legs should be about 10 cm long and the tail about 25 cm long.

John Williams from *Starting technology: machines* (Wayland Publishers Ltd)

UNIT 3

How to feed your rabbit

Make sure your rabbit's food bowl is too heavy for her to tip over. Do not use a plastic bowl. Your pet might gnaw it and hurt herself on the broken pieces.

A drip-fed water bottle with a stainless steel spout is the safest and cleanest way of giving your pet fresh water.

Keep a small piece of wood in the hutch for your rabbit to gnaw on. This will stop her teeth growing too long.

Feed your pet two small meals a day and don't put out too much food as rabbits can get very fat.

A rabbit will quickly get used to a regular feeding routine, so try and feed your pet at the same times each day.

Colin and Jacqui Hawkins from *How to Look After Your Rabbit* (Walker Books Ltd)

 Write out the sentences that are true. *(15 marks)*

1   The best food bowls for rabbits are made of plastic.

2   Rabbits' teeth go on growing.

3   Rabbits never eat more than they need.

4   You should try to feed your rabbit at the same times every day.

5   Rabbits have sharp teeth.

6   You should never give rabbits water to drink.

7   Rabbits need four large meals a day.

8   Pet rabbits should be given wood to bite and chew.

9   A rabbit's food bowl needs to be quite heavy.

10   Feed your rabbit whenever it looks hungry.

Disappearing water

Have you ever wondered what happens to the water in
wet things when they dry?

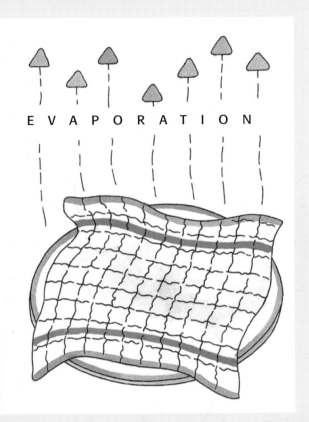

E V A P O R A T I O N

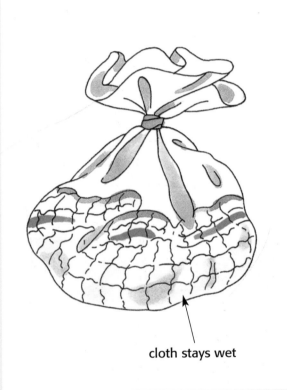

cloth stays wet

Drying out

Soak two dishcloths in water and wring them out so they are
just damp.

Spread one cloth on a plate. Put the other in a plastic bag
and tape it shut. Leave them in a warm place. Which cloth
do you think will dry first?

Feel the cloths the next day. Which one is driest?

Wet things dry out because tiny water drops escape from
them into the air. This is called evaporation.

The cloth in the bag stays wet, because the water cannot
reach the air. ⇨

Rainbow sugar

You can use evaporation to make coloured sugar crystals to eat.

You need:
2 spoons of sugar
10 spoons of water
food colour
foil dishes or saucers covered with foil

Stir the sugar into the water until it disappears.

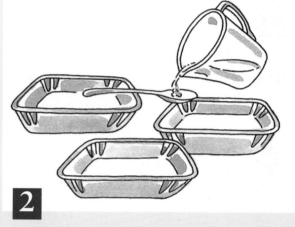

Pour two spoonfuls on to each foil dish.

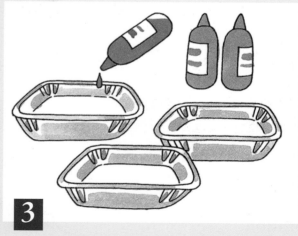

Add a different food colour to each dish.

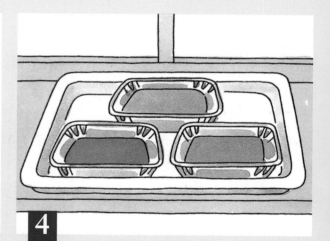

Leave the dish in a warm place for three days.

5

The water evaporates and leaves behind coloured sugar crystals.
You can break them up and mix them to make rainbow sugar.

Rebecca Heddle from *Science in the Kitchen* (Usborne Publishing Ltd)

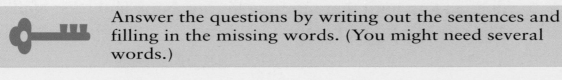

Answer the questions by writing out the sentences and
filling in the missing words. (You might need several
words.)

1   What do you do to wet things when you wring them out?
     You take them in your hands and you _____ . *(3 marks)*

2   Which of the cloths was drier the next day?
     The cloth that was _____ **was drier the next day.** *(3 marks)*

3   Where does water go when it evaporates?
     When water evaporates, it goes _____ . *(2 marks)*

4   How long does the rainbow sugar mixture take to dry out?
     It takes _____ **to dry out.** *(2 marks)*

5   Is it safe to eat the sugar when it is ready?
     It is _____ **to eat the sugar.** *(2 marks)*

6   Why is the sugar called "rainbow sugar"?
     It is called "rainbow sugar" because _____ . *(3 marks)*

UNIT 5

Luke's pet spider

"My pet is a spider. He's called Dizzy. My mum found him under my bed and I rescued him."

There was a silence. Luke sat down at his desk again.

"Is that all, Luke?"

"Yes, Miss." There wasn't really anything else to add about Dizzy. Luke had only rescued him that morning, just before school. Everyone had been told to write a piece about their pet, or a neighbour's pet. Luke's neighbour was the old lady who owned the flat where Luke and his mother lived. She had the downstairs flat which she shared with a mangy and smelly old dog. That was why she wouldn't allow Luke to have any pets. Luke didn't want to write about the old dog, and up until that morning his notebook had been blank. Then he had found Dizzy.

Luke added, "But I've brought Dizzy to show everyone."
He took a shoebox from under the desk and opened the lid carefully. Three hairy legs dangled over the side of the box, and Luke quickly shut it again.

Mrs Matthews shuddered. "I think that's enough, Luke," she said. "And I think you should let Dizzy free after the lesson. It isn't very kind to keep a spider in a box."

Linda Jennings from *Jellybaby and Other Problem Pets* (Puffin)

 Choose the correct answer to each question and write it out. *(1.5 marks each)*

1 Who was Luke talking to at the beginning of the passage?
   a) Luke was talking to Mrs Matthews.
   b) Luke was talking to the pupils in his class.
   c) Luke was talking to his teacher and everyone in the class.

2 Why did Mrs Matthews say, "Is that all, Luke?" when he sat down?
   a) She was deaf.
   b) She was glad he had finished.
   c) She didn't think he had said enough.

3 How long had Luke had his pet spider?
   a) Luke had had the spider for a few hours.
   b) Luke had had the spider for a few days.
   c) Luke had had the spider for a few months.

4 How did Luke get his spider?
   a) Luke bought his spider at a pet shop.
   b) Luke's mother found the spider under his bed.
   c) Luke rescued the spider from a bird in the garden.

5 Why wouldn't the lady who lived downstairs let Luke have a pet?

   a) She didn't like animals.

   b) She thought it would smell.

   c) She didn't want to upset her dog.

6 Why didn't Luke write about his neighbour's pet?

   a) He didn't have a neighbour.

   b) His neighbour didn't have a pet.

   c) He didn't want to.

7 Why did Luke shut the shoebox lid quickly when he started
   to show his spider to the class?

   a) He thought the spider might escape.

   b) He didn't want anyone to see the spider.

   c) He didn't want to frighten Mrs Matthews.

8 Why did Mrs Matthews shudder when she saw the spider's legs?

   a) She was sorry for the spider.

   b) She was frightened of spiders.

   c) She didn't like boys.

9 What does "dangled" mean?

   a) "Dangled" means "kicked fiercely".

   b) "Dangled" means "crept slowly".

   c) "Dangled" means "hung loosely".

10 What is the plural of box?

   a) "Boxs" is the plural of "box".

   b) "Box's" is the plural of "box".

   c) "Boxes" is the plural of "box".

I am better than you

One day on a vine, a lizard named Sam met a lizard named Pete.

"Get out of my way!" said Sam.

"Why?" asked Pete.

"Because," said Sam, "I am the best lizard there is!"

"Why?" asked Pete.

"Why what?" asked Sam.

"Why are you the best lizard there is?" asked Pete.

"Because I am!" said Sam.

"But you look just like me," said Pete.

"No," said Sam. "I am pretty. You are not."

"Oh," said Pete. "I did not see that."

"I am much better than you," said Sam. "I can do things that you cannot do."

"Like what?" asked Pete.

"I can catch a fly," said Sam.

Zap! Sam got a fly.

"I can do that," said Pete.

Zop! Pete got a fly too.

Robert Lopshire from *I Am Better Than You*
(World's Work Ltd)

 Answer in sentences. (*3 marks each*)

1   Why did Sam think he was better than Pete?

2   What could Pete do just as well as Sam?

3   Which of the following words describes Sam best?
    friendly   boastful   hungry

4   Is it true that Pete believed everything that Sam said?

5   Write down three words from the passage that rhyme with "fly".

UNIT 7

The smallest bird in the world and the largest bird in the world

The smallest bird in the world

The smallest bird in the world is the bee humming bird. This bird comes from Cuba, which is an island near America. All humming birds are small, but this one is very small. It is about as long as your little finger. It is called a bee humming bird because it is not much bigger than a bee.

Humming birds are different from other birds in the way they fly. They move their wings so fast that you can hardly see them. The wings make a humming sound and that is how the birds get their name.

The humming bird is like a little helicopter. Helicopters can stay in one place in the air. This is called hovering. Most other birds are like aeroplanes. Once they are in the air they have to keep going forwards. But a humming bird can hover in one place and fly backwards as well as forwards, just like a helicopter.

The largest bird in the world

The largest bird in the world is the ostrich. Most ostriches live in Africa. An ostrich is as tall as a human. It is so strong that a child can sit on its back. It can run as fast as a horse and it can kick as hard as a horse, too!

An ostrich's wings are very small and it cannot fly. But it uses its wings to help it to keep its balance when it runs fast.

from *New Caribbean Junior Reader 2* (Ginn & Co)

 Answer in sentences.

1   What part of a humming bird makes a humming noise? *(1 mark)*

2   What do ostriches use their wings for? *(2 marks)*

3   Write down two ways in which a humming bird is like a helicopter. *(4 marks)*

4   Write down two ways in which an ostrich is like a horse. *(4 marks)*

5   Why are the smallest kind of humming birds called bee humming birds? *(2 marks)*

6   In which country would you see bee humming birds flying around? *(1 mark)*

7   Where do most ostriches live? *(1 mark)*

Sally

Peter was playing the piano with Sally sitting beside him. She looked as alert and intelligent as black-and-white collies always do. Peter looked sideways at her.

"Anyone would think you wanted to play," he said. "Do you?" The dog sat silent, watching his face.

"Well," said Peter. "Speak when you're spoken to." Sally growled. "All right," said Peter. "Shut the door then, Sal," and at these words the collie jumped off the piano stool and ran across the room to the open door. She leapt up and put her front paws against it so that it slammed shut.

These tricks were useful ones, Peter found. When he said, "Shut the door" he didn't have to get up if he was lying reading. When he said "Speak when you're spoken to" Sally growled and got rid of unwanted visitors. The louder he said it, the fiercer Sally growled and the quicker they went.

"For a dog like Sally, piano-playing should be a piece of cake," thought Peter. "Up!" he said to her, and she jumped on to the stool, and "Sit!" and she sat. Peter took a bit of biscuit out of his pocket and held it in front of her but out of reach.

"Play the piano!" he said. Sally did not move. "Play the piano!" said Peter again, and he brought the biscuit down and nearer, and kept saying it and kept lowering it until at last the collie could bear it no longer. She put her front paws on the keyboard and took the biscuit from Peter's fingers.

"Good dog!" said Peter, as a horrible crashing discord rang out.

Dick King-Smith from *Sally*
(Ginn & Company)

Write out the sentences that are true. *(15 marks)*

1   Sally didn't really like Peter very much.

2   Peter would have preferred to have a cat.

3   Sally closed the door whenever Peter asked.

4   Sally talked by growling whenever Peter asked.

5   Sally played the piano very well.

6   Sally made a terrible noise when she put her paws on the piano keyboard.

7   Peter taught Sally to play all the tunes he knew.

8   Sally was a black-and-white collie dog.

9   Sally loved eating the cake that Peter kept in his pocket.

10 Peter thought Sally was very intelligent.

UNIT 9

Making nettle paper

You can make paper from common stinging nettles.

You will need:

lots of nettle leaves
a pair of scissors
a sieve
newspapers

an old large saucepan
a plastic bucket
gardening gloves

1

2

3

4

John and Dorothy Paull from *Simple Chemistry* (Ladybird Junior Science)

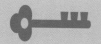 Write out the instructions in the correct order to explain how to make nettle paper. *(2.5 marks each)*

Drain the water out of the bucket and ask a grown-up to boil the leaves in a saucepan half full of water until they turn a pale yellow colour. Leave them in the saucepan until the water is cool.

Put on the gardening gloves and pull about 50 leaves off some stinging nettle plants.

Scoop the leaves out of the saucepan with a sieve and spread them out carefully on some newspaper on a flat surface. The fibres of the nettle leaves will bind together as they dry to make a sheet of thick, yellowy paper.

Cover the damp "paper" with more newspapers and press with two or three heavy books.

Remove your handmade sheet of paper after two days.

Keeping your gloves on, carefully cut the stinging nettle leaves into small pieces and soak them in a bucket of cold water for two or three days.

Dragon breath

Just around breakfast time, shortly after Vera had returned from her daily jog in the forest, Snap shuffled into the kitchen, sat himself down in a chair, and glowered at his nose. As if he was annoyed with it.

"Snap, what *are* you doing?" asked Vera, pouring herself some carrot juice.

"I'm practising," replied Snap, breathing out through his nose whilst frowning at his nostrils.

Vera looked puzzled. "Practising what?"

"Breathing fire," replied Snap.

He took a deep breath, and frowned at his nostrils even harder than before. Suddenly, he sat back in his chair, stared up at the ceiling, and let his shoulders droop.

"What's the use," he groaned. "It's no good. I can't do it." He turned to Vera sadly. "I haven't breathed *any* fire since my birthday, you know. Not even the tiniest little bit." He stuck out his bottom lip, closed his eyes and started sniffing to himself, quietly. The way he did when he was about to burst into tears.

"Never mind," said Vera quickly – she hated it when Snap cried, his dragon tears stained the carpet. "Who wants to breathe fire anyway? That's what I always say."

"I do," sniffed Snap.

"Why?"

"Because I'm a dragon – and that's what dragons do. Boo-hoo-hoo."

Stan Cullimore from *Snap, the Superhero* (Piccadilly Press)

20

🔑━ᶦᵘ Answer in sentences.

1   Why was Snap unhappy? *(2 marks)*

2   "Snap shuffled into the kitchen." (line 2). How do you walk if
     you shuffle? *(2 marks)*

3   What two things do you learn about Vera that make you think she
     liked to be fit and healthy? *(2 marks)*

4   Why did Snap want to breathe fire? *(1 mark)*

5   What two signs always showed that Snap was going to cry? *(2 marks)*

6   Why did Vera not want Snap to cry? *(2 marks)*

7   If you were Vera, what would you say to cheer Snap up? *(4 marks)*

Mrs Goat and her seven little kids

Once upon a time, Big Mother Goat was about to go to the supermarket.

"Kids," she said to her children, "don't you open that door to ANYONE. If you do, the hungry wolf will probably get in, and eat you all. Now, we don't want that, do we?"

"No, we don't want that," said the kids.

"I'll kick him on the leg!" shouted the littlest one.

Now the wolf was hiding underneath the window, and he heard all this. When Big Mother Goat had gone on her way, he knocked on the door.

"Who's that?" shouted the kids together.

"I'm your mum," the wolf growled. "Open up the door, I forgot to give you your pocket money."

"You're not Mum," shouted the littlest one. "Mum's got a squeaky little voice that sounds like music."

"You're the Hungry Wolf," shouted the kids, and they wouldn't open the door.

So the wolf ran off to the music teacher's house.

"Teach me to speak in a squeaky little voice, like music," he growled. "If you don't, I'll bite your beak off."

"Very well," said the music teacher, and she did her best.

Then the wolf hurried back to the kids' house, and banged on the door. "Let me in, this is Mummy, I've got some sweets for you," he called.

"Show us your hoof first," said the littlest one, and the wolf pushed his paw through the letterbox.

Tony Ross from *Mrs Goat and Her Seven Little Kids* (Andersen Press)

  Answer in sentences.

1 Which word in the passage means "young goats"? *(2 marks)*

2 Why couldn't the goats open the door to anyone while their mother was out? *(2 marks)*

3 How did the Hungry Wolf try to trick them into opening the door the first time he knocked? *(2 marks)*

4 How did the little goats know he was not their mother? *(2 marks)*

5 How did the Hungry Wolf try to trick them the second time? *(2 marks)*

6 How do you think the little goats will know he is not their mother this time? *(2 marks)*

7 Think of three words that would describe the smallest and youngest goat. He seems to have a lot to say! *(3 marks)*

Bird beaks

If you find a bird skull, or a dead bird, the shape of the beak will tell you what sort of food the bird ate.

Grey heron

Tawny owl

Mallard

Reed warbler

Hawfinch

Meat eater. All birds of prey have hooked beaks used for tearing meat.

Seed eater. All finches have strong, stubby beaks used for cracking open seeds and nuts.

Tiny plants and animals are caught on the grooves on the margin of the beak as water is passed through the bill.

Insect eater. Has a thin, pointed beak used for catching flying insects.

Fish eater. Has a long, sharp beak used for stabbing fish and water animals.

Alfred Leutscher from *The Spotter's Guide to Animals, Tracks and Signs* (Usborne Publishing Ltd)

 Work out which beak description belongs to each bird and answer the questions in sentences. *(3 marks each)*

1   What do grey herons eat?

2   What do reed warblers eat?

3   What do hawfinches eat?

4   What do mallard eat?

5   Is a tawny owl a meat eater, a seed eater, a fish eater or a plant eater?

UNIT 13

Fiction

Mrs Cockle

Old Mrs Cockle lived at the top of a very tall house in London. Most of the people who knew her were sorry for her, because she had to climb eighty-four stairs before she reached her own front-door; but she did not mind. It is true that all that climbing made the backs of her knees ache, but then there were advantages.

26

Mrs Cockle lived so high that, from her window, she had a view of the sky over the top of the tall house opposite – which was more than most people had. In the mornings she could look out and think, The sky is blue all over – I'll wear my straw bonnet today; or, The sky is white with snow coming – I'll wear my woollen shawl today; or, The sky has clouded right over – I'll take my biggest umbrella. Mrs Cockle had three umbrellas for different weathers, and the biggest of the three was larger than umbrellas are ever made nowadays.

There was another advantage for Mrs Cockle in living at the very top of the house. In the middle of her ceiling there was a trapdoor, and, if she set up her step-ladder underneath it, she could climb up, open the trapdoor, and climb through on to the roof itself.

Philippa Pearce from *Mrs Cockle's Cat* (Puffin)

 **Answer in sentences.**

1 How did Mrs Cockle feel about having to climb so many stairs? *(2 marks)*

2 Why did Mrs Cockle like living at the top of the house? Give as many reasons as you can. *(3 marks)*

3 Why did Mrs Cockle need three umbrellas? *(2 marks)*

4 What did Mrs Cockle wear when the sky was blue? *(2 marks)*

5 What did Mrs Cockle wear when the sky was white? *(2 marks)*

6 What do the following words mean? *(1 mark each)*
   a) **advantage**
   b) **bonnet**
   c) **shawl**
   d) **trapdoor**

U N I T
14

Children's library guide

How do I join the library?

Ask for a form. Get your Mum or Dad to fill it in and sign it. Take it back to the library.

If your library is computerised, you will be given one ticket; if not, you will have up to eight tickets or tokens. REMEMBER: it costs nothing and anybody can join, however young.

How many books can I have?

You can have up to eight.

How long can I keep them?

For up to four weeks. If you want to keep them longer, either bring them back to the library, or telephone. We can let you keep the books for another four weeks if no one else wants them. REMEMBER: bringing your books back on time will save you a fine.

What sort of books are there?

Picture Books Easy Reading Books   Story Books

Information Books   Story Cassettes

Most libraries have small reference sections to help you with your homework.

How do I find the books I want?

Story books are in A-Z order of the writer's last name.

Information books are given subject numbers. The books are put on the shelves in number order. There is a list of the subject numbers in the library called "Where's that Book?"

Can I ask for a book to be kept for me?

Yes! If you can't find the book you want, you may reserve the book by filling in a request card. This card will be sent to you when the book is ready to collect.

What else happens in the library?

Ask about storytimes, holiday activities and talks.

REMEMBER: if you need any help - ask the librarian.

Devon County Libraries Children's Guide (Devon County Council)

Choose the correct answer to each question and write it out. *(1.5 marks each)*

1   Who should sign the form when you join the library?

    a) You should sign the form yourself when you join the library.
    b) A parent should sign the form when you join the library.
    c) The librarian should sign the form when you join the library.

2   How much does it cost to join the library?

    a) It costs £1 to join the library.
    b) It costs as much as you can afford to join the library.
    c) It costs nothing to join the library.

3   How many books can you borrow at a time from this library?

    a) You can borrow eight books at a time from this library.
    b) You can borrow six books at a time from this library.
    c) You can borrow as many books as you like at a time from this library.

4   How long can you keep the books for?

    a) You can keep the books for two weeks.
    b) You can keep the books for four weeks.
    c) You can keep the books for six weeks.

5   Can someone who is three years old join this library?

    a) No, someone who is three can't join this library.
    b) Yes, someone who is three can join this library.
    c) Someone who is three can join this library if they can read.

6   What can you borrow as well as books?

    a) You can borrow cassettes.
    b) You can borrow jigsaws.
    c) You can borrow comics.

7   There are books by the following writers in the library.
     Which writer comes nearest the beginning of the story section?
     Anne Fine
     Gene Kemp
     Roald Dahl

     a) Roald Dahl comes nearest the beginning of the story section.
     b) Gene Kemp comes nearest the beginning of the story section.
     c) Anne Fine comes nearest the beginning of the story section.

8   What happens if you don"t return your books on time?

     a) You have to pay some money to the library.
     b) You have to buy the books.
     c) You are not allowed to come to the library again.

9   Which word means: "arrange for a book to be kept especially
     for you"?

     **a) "Reference" means "arrange for a book to be kept especially
        for you".**
     **b) "Request" means "arrange for a book to be kept especially
        for you".**
     **c) "Reserve" means "arrange for a book to be kept especially
        for you".**

10   What is the plural of "library"?

     a) The plural of "library" is "librarys".
     b) The plural of "library" is "libraryes".
     c) The plural of "library" is "libraries".

UNIT 15

Bicycle safety

Bicycles are very fast so they can be dangerous unless they are ridden correctly. To be safe on their bicycles, cyclists should always:

- wear a helmet
  - wear brightly coloured clothes so they can be seen easily
  - use lights in the dark
    - maintain their bicycle so that the brakes work and all the parts run smoothly
  - learn the highway code and obey the rules of the road

Helmets

Cyclists should always wear a safety helmet. A helmet protects a rider's head in an accident. Without a helmet a fall from a bicycle can lead to serious head injuries. A good helmet is very light and has air holes to keep the rider cool.

Clothing

Clothing must keep a cyclist warm and dry without making him or her overheat. Bright colours are easily seen by motorists and help with safety.

Lights

Bicycle lights must be used when riding at night. The front light is white and the back light is red.

Maintenance

Regular maintenance keeps a bicycle safe and running smoothly. Brakes should be checked and worn brake blocks replaced. The chain should be cleaned and lubricated. Modern bicycle parts should not be oiled too much. The oil attracts dirt and grit which wears the parts out quickly.

Cycling proficiency

The cycling proficiency test checks children's basic cycling and road user skills. Children are trained to get on and off a bicycle safely, to give the correct signals and to obey the rules of the road. They learn how to check that their brakes are working properly and when they need lights. They must answer questions about road signs and the highway code. When they pass they receive a badge and a certificate.

Answer in sentences.

1   Why is it sensible for people to wear brightly coloured clothes when they are riding a bicycle in traffic? *(2 marks)*

2   Why should cyclists wear a safety helmet? *(2 marks)*

3   Would it be good advice or bad advice if someone told you to oil your bicycle every day? Why? *(2 marks)*

4   Give three reasons why it is a good idea to pass your cycling proficiency test before you ride a bicycle in traffic. *(6 marks)*

5   Which bicycle light is red, the front or the back light? *(1 mark)*

6   Which word in the passage means "keeping in good working order"? *(1 mark)*

7   What word could you use instead of "lubricated" in the following sentence?
The chain should be cleaned and lubricated. *(1 mark)*

Fiction: modern fairy tale

Beware, Princess!

Poppy was a princess, but she didn't feel
like one. Her parents were a King and Queen
and they lived in a castle so she knew she must be a princess.
But Poppy had read a lot about princesses, and she knew
what they were supposed to be like. They should have long
blonde hair, blue eyes and pink cheeks. Poppy had short
black hair and brown eyes. She spent as much time out of
doors as she could, so her face was nice and brown too.

Princesses in books always wore beautiful dresses.
Poppy was rather scruffy and though she *had* some
beautiful dresses, they always seemed to end up torn and
dirty. Beautiful dresses are no good if you like to play
outdoors a lot.

For the first nine years of her life, Poppy more or less
had her own way. Although the King and Queen were
perhaps a little disappointed by her, she was a great favourite
with the castle guards, the cook and the gardener. Then on
her ninth birthday, after a really royal tea – there were *some*
advantages in being a princess – her parents took her aside
for a serious talk.

"Now, my dear," said the King, "as you are the only heir
to our throne, your mother and I thought it was time for you
to start on some of your princessly duties."

"Bother," thought Poppy, "I suppose I'll have to stop
enjoying myself now. And I know I'll be no good at them."

Out loud, she said, "Yes, Father, but what *are* my
princessly duties?"

The King began to look vague. "Well," he said.

"Don't beat about the bush, Algy," interrupted the
Queen. "Tell her about the ogre!"

34

"You see, my dear," said the King, "we have an ogre in the kingdom, of rather ... er ... *traditional* tastes."

"Traditional be blowed," said the Queen, rather rudely. "The point is, Poppy, that like most ogres, his taste is for princesses."

"To play with?" asked Poppy innocently.

"To eat," said her mother.

Mary Hoffman from *Beware, Princess!* (Mammoth)

🔑 Answer in sentences.

1 What colour were Poppy's eyes? *(2 marks)*

2 Did Poppy have long hair or short hair? *(2 marks)*

3 Why did Poppy's dresses get so torn and dirty? *(2 marks)*

4 What do the following words and phrases mean? *(1 mark each)*
   a) advantage
   b) heir to the throne
   c) beat about the bush
   d) interrupt
   e) ogre
   f) innocent

5 The passage comes from a story called "Beware, Princess!" Why do you think it is called that? *(3 marks)*

UNIT 17

The lion and his three counsellors

A lion called a sheep to him and asked her if his breath smelt.

"Yes," she replied, and he killed her for her foolishness.

He then called a wolf and asked the same question.

"No, not at all," replied the wolf, but he fared no better, for the lion tore him to pieces, calling him a flatterer.

Finally the lion asked a fox his opinion on the matter.

"I have a bad cold," crafty Reynard replied, "and can smell nothing at all."

Wise men keep a guard on their tongues.

Aesop

Answer in sentences.
Some of the answers have been started for you.

1   What was the actual question that the lion asked the sheep? *(2 marks)*
    The lion asked the sheep, "Does... "

2   In what way was the sheep foolish? *(2 marks)*

3   Why did the lion kill the wolf? *(2 marks)*

4   Explain how the fox was being very clever when he said he had a cold. *(3 marks)*

5   What do the following words mean? *(1 mark each)*
    a) flatterer
    b) crafty
    c) finally

6   Explain the moral of the story in your own words. *(3 marks)*
    "Wise men keep a guard on their tongues" means...

Uninvited ghosts

Marian and Simon were sent to bed early on the day that the Brown family moved house. By then everyone had lost their temper with everyone else; the cat had been sick on the sitting-room carpet; the dog had run away twice. If you have ever moved you will know what kind of day it had been. Packing cases and newspapers all over the place ... sandwiches instead of proper meals ... the kettle lost and a wardrobe stuck on the stairs and Mrs Brown's favourite vase broken. There was bread and baked beans for supper, the television wouldn't work and the water wasn't hot so when all was said and done the children didn't object too violently to being packed off to bed. They'd had enough, too. They had one last argument about who was going to sleep by the window, put on their pyjamas, got into bed, switched the lights out ... and it was at that point that the ghost came out of the bottom drawer of the chest of drawers.

It oozed out, a grey cloudy shape about three feet long smelling faintly of woodsmoke, sat down on a chair and began to hum to itself. It looked like a bundle of bedclothes, except that it was not solid: you could see, quite clearly, the cushion on the chair beneath it. ⇨

37

Marian gave a shriek. "That's a ghost!"

"Oh, be quiet, dear, do," said the ghost. "That noise goes right through my head. And it's not nice to call people names." It took out a ball of wool and some needles and began to knit.

What would you have done? Well, yes – Simon and Marian did just that and I daresay you can imagine what happened. You try telling your mother that you can't get to sleep because there's a ghost sitting in the room clacking its knitting-needles and humming. Mrs Brown said the kind of things she could be expected to say and the ghost continued sitting there knitting and humming and Mrs Brown went out, banging the door and saying threatening things about if there's so much as another word from either of you ...

"She can't see it," said Marian to Simon.

"Course not, dear," said the ghost. "It's the kiddies I'm here for. Love kiddies, I do. We're going to be ever such friends."

"Go away!" yelled Simon. "This is our house now!"

"No, it isn't," said the ghost smugly. "Always been here, I have. A hundred years and more. Seen plenty of families come and go, I have. Go to bye-byes now, there's good children."

The children glared at it and buried themselves under the bedclothes. And, eventually, slept.

The next night it was there again. This time it was smoking a long white pipe and reading a newspaper dated 1842. Beside it was a second grey cloudy shape. "Hello, dearies," said the ghost. "Say how do you do to my Auntie Edna."

"She can't come here too," wailed Marian.

"Oh yes she can," said the ghost. "Always comes here in August, does Auntie. She likes a change."

Penelope Lively from *A Treasury of Stories for Eight-year-olds*, eds. Edward and Nancy Blishen (Kingfisher Books)

 Answer in sentences.

1 What did the Browns lose in the move? *(1 mark)*

2 What was broken? *(1 mark)*

3 What did the Brown family have for supper? *(1 mark)*

4 What did the cat do that made people cross? *(1 mark)*

5 Why did Mr and Mrs Brown send Marian and Simon to bed early? *(1.5 marks)*

6 How did Marian and Simon feel when they were sent to bed early? *(1.5 marks)*

7 The ghost was not very frightening but it was very annoying. Write down two annoying things that it did. *(2 marks)*

8 Why didn't Mrs Brown believe the children when they told her about the ghost? *(2 marks)*

9 How do we know that the Browns moved into a house that is at least one hundred years old? *(2 marks)*

10 Which word tells us that Marian was really miserable when she saw two ghosts in the bedroom on the second night? *(2 marks)*

UNIT

19

The magic finger

The farm next to ours is owned by Mr and Mrs Gregg. The Greggs have two children, both of them boys. Their names are Philip and William. Sometimes I go over to their farm to play with them.

I am a girl and I am eight years old.

Philip is also eight years old.

William is three years older. He is ten.

What?

Oh, all right, then.

He is eleven.

Last week, something very funny happened to the Gregg family. I am going to tell you about it as best I can.

Now the one thing that Mr Gregg and his two boys loved to do more than anything else was to go hunting. Every Saturday morning they would take their guns and go off into the woods to look for animals and birds to shoot. Even Philip, who was only eight years old, had a gun of his own.

I can't stand hunting. I just can't *stand* it. It doesn't seem right to me that men and boys should kill animals just for the fun they get out of it. So I used to try to stop Philip and William from doing it. Every time I went over to their farm I would do my best to talk them out of it, but they only laughed at me.

I even said something about it once to Mr Gregg, but he just walked on past me as if I weren't there.

Then, one Saturday morning, I saw Philip and William coming out of the woods with their father and they were carrying a lovely young deer.

This made me so cross that I started shouting at them.

The boys laughed and made faces at me, and Mr Gregg told me to go home and mind my own P's and Q's.

Well, that did it!

I saw red.

And before I was able to stop myself, I did something I never meant to do.

I PUT THE MAGIC FINGER ON THEM ALL!

Roald Dahl from *The Magic Finger* (Puffin)

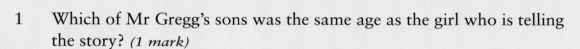

Answer in sentences.

1   Which of Mr Gregg's sons was the same age as the girl who is telling the story? *(1 mark)*

2   What job did Mr Gregg do? *(2 marks)*

3   How do you know that the girl and the two boys were friends? *(2 marks)*

4   What did Mr Gregg and his sons love doing every Saturday morning? *(1 mark)*

5   The girl didn't like what Mr Gregg and his sons did so she tried to "talk them out of it". What does "talk them out of it" mean? *(2 marks)*

6   How did the girl feel when she saw they had killed a young deer? *(2 marks)*

7   How do we know that the boys weren't at all sorry for what they had done? *(2 marks)*

8   What strange thing did the girl say she did to the Greggs before she could stop herself? *(1 mark)*

9   This passage comes from the opening of a book. Do you think it would make people want to read the rest of the book to find out what happens next? Why? *(2 marks)*

UNIT 20

Life's not been the same in my family

Life's not been the same in my family
since the day that the new baby came,
my parents completely ignore me,
they scarcely remember my name.

The baby gets all their attention,
"Oh, isn't she precious!" they croon,
they think that she looks like an angel,
I thinks she resembles a prune.

They're thrilled when she giggles and gurgles,
"She burped!" they exclaim with delight,
they don't even mind when she wakes us
with deafening screams in the night.

They seem to believe she's a treasure,
there's simply no way I agree,
I wish she'd stop being a baby
and start being older than me.

Jack Prelutsky from *Something Big Has Been Here* (William Heinemann)

 Choose the correct answer to each question and write it out.

1   How did the girl feel about the new baby in her family? *(3 marks)*

a) **The girl was jealous of the new baby.**
b) **The girl loved the new baby.**
c) **The girl kept forgetting the new baby was there.**

2   In what way did the baby look like a prune? *(2 marks)*

    a) She was the same colour as a prune.

    b) She was small and wrinkled like a prune.

    c) She looked good enough to eat.

3   How have the parents behaved since the new baby was born? *(2 marks)*

    a) They have made a great fuss of both of their children.

    b) They have paid no attention to the baby.

    c) They have paid no attention to their older daughter.

4   Why does the girl say,
*"I wish she'd stop being a baby
and start being older than me"*? *(2 marks)*

    a) She wants an older sister to play with.

    b) She thinks the only way of getting any attention is to be the youngest child.

    c) She feels sorry for the baby being so young.

5   Which pair of words rhymes? *(2 marks)*

    a) giggles gurgles

    b) croon prune

    c) simply resembles

6   What does "scarcely" mean in verse one? *(2 marks)*

    a) never

    b) always

    c) hardly

7   What does "exclaim" mean in verse three? *(2 marks)*

    a) whisper

    b) shout

    c) ask

Years of compulsory education

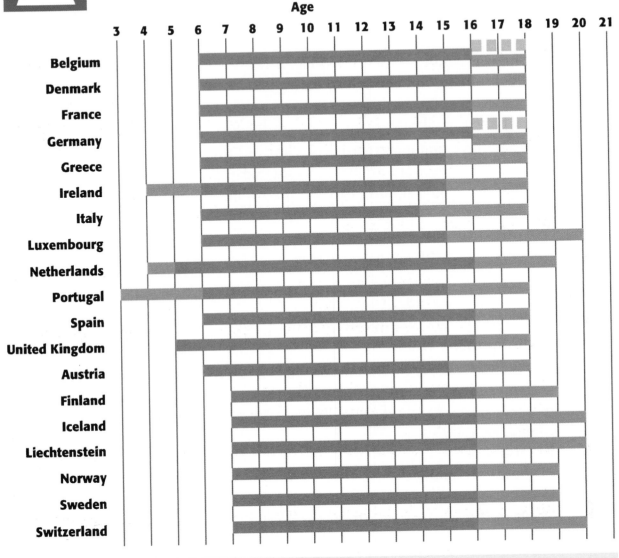

Key

compulsory full-time

voluntary full-time

compulsory part-time

Glossary

Compulsory education: children have to attend school by law

Voluntary education: children may attend school if they choose

1   In Italy, children can leave school when they are _____ years old.
    (1 mark)

2   In the Netherlands and the United Kingdom children must go to school
    when they are _____ years old and can leave school when they
    are _____ years old. *(2 marks)*

3   In Ireland, children can start school at the age of _____ but it is
    not compulsory until they are _____. *(1 mark)*

4   Children in the United Kingdom have to attend school for _____
    years more than children in Austria. *(1 mark)*

5   _____ countries in the table have a school leaving age of fifteen.
    (1 mark)

6   Compulsory education begins at the age of _____
    or _____ in most countries in the table. *(2 marks)*

7   In Portugal, children can start school at the age of _____ but
    it is not compulsory until they are _____. *(1 mark)*

8   Most countries in the table have a leaving age of _____. *(1 mark)*

9   In the United Kingdom, you can stay at school until the age of
    _____ if you want to. *(1 mark)*

10 In Sweden, children start school at the age of _____. *(1 mark)*

11 Two countries offer two years of voluntary part-time education
    over the age of sixteen. They are _____ and _____. *(2 marks)*

12 Pupils in Switzerland have _____ years of compulsory education.
    (1 mark)

UNIT 22

What is glass?

Glass was discovered a very long time ago, and has been used for centuries to make useful objects. Look around you and see how many things are made of glass. Windows, mirrors, bottles, jars, lenses and television screens are all made of glass.

Glass is usually a hard, brittle material. But when glass is heated, it changes. The glass melts, and runs and flows like a sticky liquid.

Molten glass can be pulled, stretched and pressed in any direction and made into different shapes.

When glass is cool, it becomes strong and hard. The glass may feel solid, but it is still really a liquid. Scientists call glass a "supercooled liquid". Like a clear liquid, glass is transparent and light passes through it. The unusual properties of glass make it a very useful material.

Hazel Songhurst from *Glass* (Wayland)

Answer in sentences.

1 Is it true that glass is really a liquid? *(1 mark)*

2 Write down six everyday glass objects that are mentioned in the passage. *(2 marks)*

3 Think of four more everyday objects made of glass and write them down. *(2 marks)*

4 Explain why glass is a very unusual material. Give all the reasons you can find in the passage. *(2 marks)*

5 What do the following words mean? *(3 marks)*

brittle   **transparent**   **properties**

6 How many years are there in a century? *(1 mark)*

7 What is the difference between a discovery and an invention? *(4 marks)*

Our playground

Our playground wouldn't be so bad
If it didn't slope so much,
But as it is, when we play football,
We have to have two sides:
The Uphills and the Downhills;
And the Uphills always lose.

Life must be as sloping as our playground;
For there always seem two sides:
The Uphills and the Downhills;
And the Uphills always lose.

Colin West from *Tough Toffee*, ed. David Orme (Lions)

 Write out the sentence from each pair that is true.
(3 marks each)

1   a) The playground is good for playing football on because it is level.
    b) The playground is no good for playing football on because it slopes.

2   a) The team that has to score at the top of the slope always loses.
    b) The team that has to score at the bottom of the slope always loses.

3   a) Both verses begin with the same line.
    b) Both verses end with the same line.

4   a) The poet thinks that life is like a fair game of football.
    b) The poet thinks that life is like a game of football played
       on a sloping playground.

5   a) In real life, the "Downhills" are lucky and successful people.
    b) In real life, the "Downhills" are football fans.

Newspaper report

BOY ATTACKED by MASTIFF...

A ten-year-old boy is recovering in hospital after being savaged by a bull mastiff just a few miles from where a youngster was killed by the same breed of dog. Mark Davison was playing with friends in a garden near his home in Stockton-on-Tees, when the chained-up dog broke free.

The boy's mother said: "The dog flung itself at Mark and knocked him over, then began attacking him. The father of the family who own the dog saw what was happening and ran to help. He pulled the dog off and it turned on him, biting him on the arm. The father called the police and ambulance and had the dog destroyed straight away."

Mark, who has cuts and bruises on his arms, face and chest, is recovering in Middlesbrough General Hospital.

From "*Early Times Newspapers*" 23/12/93-5/01/04

1   Mark Davison was ten years old when the dog attacked him.

2   The dog would not have bitten Mark if the children had left it alone.

3   Mark was playing in his garden when the dog attacked him.

4   The dog has now been destroyed.

5   The police said the dog should have been chained up.

6   Mark was injured on his face, chest and arms.

7   The dog that attacked Mark was an alsatian.

8   Nobody telephoned for an ambulance.

9   Mark's mother called the police.

10   The dog that attacked Mark bit its owner too.

11   Mark was walking quietly along the road when it happened.

12   The dog that attacked Mark had already killed a child who lived in the area.

13   Mark received treatment at Middlesbrough General Hospital.

14   The dog that attacked Mark belonged to his brother.

15   Mark's legs were injured in the attack.

UNIT 25

Albert changes schools

Albert was ten years old. He was a quiet, gentle sort of a boy with a thatch of stiff hair that he twiddled when he was nervous.

He had moved to town from the countryside. "We have to go where the work is," his mother had told him, and there was work in the town.

So Albert came from his little village school to a new school, a school which was noisy and full of strange faces. The other children called him Bert, or Herbert, neither of which was his name. They kept asking him questions and they wouldn't leave him alone.

There was somewhere to get away from it all, behind the bike shed in the playground, but never for long. By the end of each day Albert felt like a sponge squeezed dry. He smiled so much that it hurt. He tried to laugh at everyone's jokes, and he believed everything they told him. He was naturally a

trusting child, and now, in the first weeks of his new school, he wanted to please everyone, to make friends.

They teased Albert of course, and he was easy enough to tease, but Albert just smiled through it all. They called him "Twiddler!" and Albert smiled and went on twiddling his hair. He did not seem to mind.

It was Sid Creedy who discovered that Albert would believe almost anything he told him. They were playing football in the playground at break when Sid turned to his friends and said, "Watch this." He dribbled the ball over towards Albert, and his friends followed him.

"My Dad," said Sid, "he played centre-forward for Liverpool. Did for years. Then they asked him to play for England, but he didn't want to – he didn't like the colour of the shirt."

Michael Morpurgo from *The Marble Crusher* (Egmont)

 Answer in sentences.

1   Why had Albert's mother decided they had to move to the town? *(2 marks)*

2   Why was Albert nicknamed Twiddler? *(2 marks)*

3   Where did Albert go to try to hide from the other children? *(2 marks)*

4   Why did Albert smile and laugh so much at his new school? *(3 marks)*

5   How do you dribble a ball? *(3 marks)*

6   Why did Sid tell his friends to watch while he told Albert the story about his father? *(3 marks)*

U N I T

26

Dilly Dinosaur, Detective

"Hold on a second, Dilly," said Father as we were leaving for school the other morning. "Would you mind telling me *why* you're asking all these questions? It's starting to get on my nerves."

I think Mother and I felt exactly the same. Ever since he'd woken up, Dilly had been pestering the three of us with loads of amazingly stupid questions, like what was our address and where did we spend our holiday last year? He must have known the answers, so what was going on in his tiny, devious mind?

"I'm not sure if I should," said Dilly, giving Father a strange look. "I haven't finished my investigating yet..."

It took a while, but Father finally persuaded him to explain. I'd already worked it out, though. The "investigating" bit had given it away. I had realised Dilly was pretending to be a detective, and that was because of the TV programme we had watched with Mother and Father the night before.

It had been the latest episode of *Inspector Duff, Dinosaur Detective*. Inspector Duff is brilliant at solving tough cases. He does it by asking lots of questions, although occasionally he has to take drastic action to unmask a clever villain.

Tony Bradman from *Dilly Dinosaur, Detective* (Mammoth)

 Answer in sentences.

1   What was Dilly pretending to be? *(1 mark)*

2   Did Dilly explain why he was asking so many questions? *(1 mark)*

3   What is "TV" short for? *(1 mark)*

4   How did the family feel about being asked questions? *(1 mark)*

5   Why was it silly for Dilly to ask the family what their address was and where they had been on their holidays? *(2 marks)*

6   Which word in paragraph four means "in the end"? *(1 mark)*

7   Which word in the last paragraph tells us that "Inspector Duff, Dinosaur Detective" is a series of programmes and not just one programme? *(1 mark)*

8   What do the following words mean? *(1 mark each)*
   a) pester
   b) devious
   c) investigating
   d) solve
   e) occasionally
   f) unmask
   g) villain

UNIT 27

Life in a castle

A castle was not only a fortress. It was normally the home of a community of men, women, children and animals. Though a castle may be a ruin nowadays, without a roof or floors to the rooms, we must not forget that those same rooms once had the fittings, furniture and atmosphere of a home and echoed to the daily noise of a community of people.

In the Great Hall there were long trestle tables, with benches to sit on. If there were any chairs, the two largest would be placed at one end of the room to be used by the lord of the castle and his wife. Lesser people sat either on hard, wooden stools or on wooden storage chests. There were no carpets on the floors, just rushes or straw on the wooden boards or stone slabs.

In the sleeping quarters most people slept on straw mattresses on the floor. A bed was a most important and valuable piece of furniture in those days, and only the lord and his wife were likely to have one.

Sanitation in castles was relatively good, though perhaps not quite as convenient as it is made by our pipes, taps and tanks. If you wanted to take a bath, water was heated and then poured into a wooden tub (as it was until quite recent times in many houses). There were probably curtains hanging down from a pole to pull around you if you were shy or felt the draughts.

The castle lavatories, or garderobes, were generally set in small rooms built into the thick outside walls. They were reached down a short passage, so that they were apart from the living quarters. Usually there were some on each floor. There was a simple stone seat, and sewage went down a chute on the exterior wall into the moat or a convenient river or into a pit at the base of the wall.

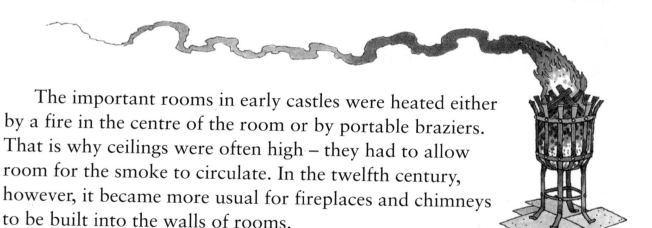

The important rooms in early castles were heated either by a fire in the centre of the room or by portable braziers. That is why ceilings were often high – they had to allow room for the smoke to circulate. In the twelfth century, however, it became more usual for fireplaces and chimneys to be built into the walls of rooms.

Hugh Gregor from *Castles: A Guide for Young People* (Macmillan for the Department of the Environment, HMSO)

 Answer in sentences.

1   What were the two main uses of a castle? *(1 mark)*

2   What was used to cover the floor? *(1 mark)*

3   What furniture would you find in the Great Hall? *(2 marks)*

4   Where did most people sleep? *(1 mark)*

5   How was having a bath different from in our times? *(2 marks)*

6   There were no flush toilets in a castle. Explain how the castle lavatories worked. *(2 marks)*

7   What is another word used in the passage that means "lavatory" or "toilet"? *(2 marks)*

8   What does "a portable brazier" mean? *(2 marks)*

9   Why did ceilings have to be high in the days when fires were in the centre of the room? *(1 mark)*

10 Write down two ways in which the lord of the castle and his wife lived a more comfortable life than other people in the castle. *(1 mark)*

UNIT

28

Hedgehogs

Introducing hedgehogs

A hedgehog is a small mammal with prickles on the back of its head and body. If it is frightened, a hedgehog curls up tightly, so that the soft parts of its body are on the inside. Few enemies can get at a hedgehog when it is curled up.

There are lots of different kinds of hedgehog. They live in Britain and the rest of Europe, right across to Russia and East China. In the hot, dry areas of Africa and Asia there are desert hedgehogs. They dig burrows to get away from the hot sun and to hide from their enemies.

Not all animals that look like hedgehogs belong to the same family. Porcupines and the Australian spiny anteater have prickles on their backs but they do not belong to the same family as the hedgehog.

How hedgehogs live

Hedgehogs live on their own. If they are with another hedgehog, it is usually because they are sharing a feeding area, such as a lawn.

Like most mammals, hedgehogs have their own special smell. The hedgehog's smell is quite strong. A hedgehog can tell the age of another hedgehog by its smell, and whether it is a male or a female. Usually a hedgehog's smell warns other hedgehogs to keep out of its way.

What hedgehogs look like

The hedgehog's spines, or prickles, are like stiff hairs. Each spine is about 22 mm long. Older hedgehogs have more spines than younger ones. A young hedgehog's spines are shiny and in good condition, but the spines of an old hedgehog are often damaged.

A hedgehog uses a special set of muscles to raise and lower its prickles. When it is frightened, a hedgehog tightens the muscles around its sides. This is how it curls up. A hedgehog can stay curled up for a long time without getting tired.

A hedgehog's small bright eyes are not very good at seeing things. A hedgehog uses its good sense of smell and hearing to find its way around.

Joanna Jessop from *Hedgehogs* (Wayland)

1   What do hedgehogs do when they are scared? *(1 mark)*

2   Give two reasons why desert hedgehogs in Africa and Asia dig burrows in the sand. *(2 marks)*

3   What two things can a hedgehog tell about another hedgehog just by its smell? *(2 marks)*

4   Make a list of four facts about a hedgehog's spines that you learn from the passage. *(4 marks)*

5   Write out the sentences that are true. *(3 marks)*

   a) Porcupines belong to the hedgehog family.

   b) Young hedgehogs have more spines than old hedgehogs.

   c) Hedgehogs cannot see very well.

   d) Hedgehogs do not have a very strong smell.

   e) Hedgehogs live in large groups.

   f) Hedgehogs are mammals

   g) Every hedgehog's colour is different.

   h) Hedgehogs curl up by tightening special muscles.

6   What do the following words mean? *(1.5 marks)*
   a) damaged
   b) desert
   c) mammal

7   Give the opposites of the following words. *(1.5 marks)*
   a) different
   b) raise
   c) old

Helen Keller

Helen Keller was born in America in 1880. When she was nearly two years old, she became seriously ill with fever. Everyone thought she would die. Helen lived, however, but when the fever finally left her she was blind and deaf. This meant that she could not see or hear how people talked, and so she couldn't learn to speak.

Helen's family loved her, but they didn't know how to help her and so they just spoiled her.

When Helen was six, a teacher named Anne Sullivan came to live with the family to try to teach Helen. Anne Sullivan had been blind too, when she was a girl. She had gone to a school for blind children and learned how to read and write Braille, the special kind of writing that blind people use. She also learned sign language. While she was at school she got back some of her sight.

When Anne Sullivan came to work with Helen, Helen was extremely spoiled and very wild. Helen had only ever known her own family and she did not like having a stranger, Anne, in the house. She fought against her furiously. Anne knew that she could not teach Helen anything until Helen learned to behave. It was a big problem, but Anne was patient with her. In the end Helen got used to Anne and began to learn to behave. Gradually, she became ready to learn more. ⇨

Anne started to teach her some words. The only way Helen could learn was through her hands, and so Anne spelled the names of things into Helen's hands, using the sign language alphabet. She made the letters with her fingers in Helen's hand so that Helen could feel them. Helen learned the word patterns fast.

But Helen did not understand what words were, because she had not learned any words before she lost her sight and hearing. The sign language words that she learned to spell out were only a game to Helen and did not mean anything to her.

Then one hot day Anne took her to the water pump. She pumped some cool water over Helen's hand. As she did this, she patiently spelled the word w-a-t-e-r in Helen's hand, over and over again. Suddenly Helen understood. The word in her hand was the name of the cool thing she was feeling! At last she understood that everything has a name. From then on, Helen learned very fast. She learned to read and write in Braille and she talked with her hands in sign language. After a time she even learned to speak. She and her teacher became famous because no one who was blind and deaf had ever learned so much before.

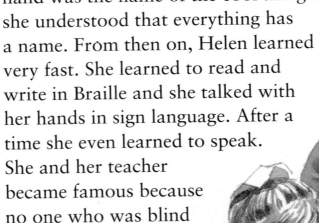

Later on, Helen Keller went to university and learned other languages besides English. She became a famous writer and she travelled all over the world to help and encourage blind people.

Peggy Campbell from *New Caribbean Junior Reader 2* (Ginn & Company)

 **Write out the sentences that are true.** *(15 marks)*

1   Helen Keller was blind and deaf when Anne Sullivan came to live with her.

2   Helen was the sweetest little girl Anne had ever met.

3   Helen was six when she lost her sight and hearing.

4   Anne Sullivan had been blind and deaf when she was young but she got her sight and hearing back.

5   Sign language is a language you talk with your hands.

6   Anne Sullivan wasn't really a teacher.

7   Anne taught Helen to read and write in Braille.

8   Helen eventually learned to speak.

9   The first word that Helen understood was "hot".

10   Helen learned new words very slowly.

11   Helen Keller became a famous dancer.

12   Helen did a great deal in her life to help other blind people.

UNIT 30

The flood

The shed was near the house. It was dark because it had only one small window, and that was covered with cobwebs. There were some tools in the shed, a spade and a rake and a hoe and a pile of old sacks. There was something else as well, that not many people knew about. If you stood quite still in the shed, without moving a hand or a foot, you could hear the crackle of straw and perhaps a tiny cry.

The crackle of straw and the cry came from a box standing in a corner. In the box were a mother cat and her three newborn kittens. The cat's name was Minnie and her kittens were named One, Two and Three. When they were big and could wash themselves and drink milk from a saucer, they would go to homes of their own. Then someone would give them proper names. But One, Two and Three did very well to start with.

Sometimes a dog barked.

"What is that?" asked One, his little legs shaking.

"It is only Prince, the dog," purred Minnie. "He is taking care of us. He barks when he sees a stranger coming."

Sometimes a door banged.

"What is that?" mewed Two, shuddering like a jelly.

"It is only the wind blowing the door shut," purred Minnie. "Now the wind won't get into our snug bed."

Sometimes the coalman tipped the coal out with a sound like thunder.

"What is that?" cried Three, hiding her face in her mother's fur.

"It is only the coalman," purred Minnie. "His coal will make the kitchen fire blaze and burn. I will take you into the kitchen for a treat, when you are bigger, if you are very good."

A lady named Mrs Plum lived in the kitchen. She wore a white apron. Every day she brought Minnie's meals to her, in a blue dish. When Minnie had finished her food, the dish was as clean as if it had been washed.

One night, when the kittens were fast asleep, curled like furry balls beside their mother, a storm blew up. The door and window of the shed rattled. The rain fell in floods on the roof. There were terrible claps of thunder and bright, zig-zag flashes of lightning. Even Minnie felt frightened. The river ran at the bottom of the garden, on the other side of the garden wall, and she could hear it roaring by. It sounded like a fierce, growling animal.

"What is wrong? What has happened?" mewed One, Two and Three.

"I do not know, my dears," said Minnie. "But we must go to sleep and not be frightened."

But Minnie herself was very frightened and so were the three kittens. No one could get to sleep while the storm was raging.   ⇨

The kittens were so young that their eyes were not yet open. But Minnie's eyes shone like green lamps. She could see, under the door of the shed, a trickle of water. The trickle grew into a puddle. The puddle grew into a wave. The wave came nearer and nearer across the floor. Then it reached the box in the corner.

Ruth Ainsworth from "The Flood" in *A Sackful of Stories for Eight-year-olds,* ed. Pat Thompson (Corgi)

 Answer in sentences. *(1.5 marks each)*

1   Why were the kittens called One, Two and Three?

2   How can you tell that One was really frightened when he heard Prince barking?

3   Is Two a female kitten?

4   Why couldn't the kittens see?

5   What had been put in the box to make it cosy for Minnie and her kittens?

6   What noise did the river make in the storm?

7   Which word in the passage means "cosy"?

8   Which word best describes Minnie?
     protective   noisy   careless

9   Which word best describes the kittens?
     jealous   timid   bold

10   What is the plural of "lady"?

Maths dictionary

parallel   lines that are parallel are the same distance apart for the whole of their length

parallelogram   a four-sided flat figure with opposite sides that are parallel and equal in length, and with equal opposite angles

pattern   a sequence of numbers or shapes repeated or changed in the same way every time
e.g.   1, 3, 5, 7, 9, 11, 13, 15, 17, 19
       3, 6, 9, 12, 15, 18, 21, 24, 27

pentagon   a flat shape with five sides and five angles

percentage   an amount expressed as part of a whole which is 100
e.g. ½ as a percentage is 50%

place value   the value of the position a digit occupies in a numeral

     e.g. 2934
       4 (units)
       3 (tens)
       9 (hundreds)
       2 (thousands)

predict   say what is coming next or what the answer will be
e.g. by analysing the pattern of a sequence

prime number   a number that can be divided exactly by only two numbers: itself and 1

product   the answer obtained by multiplying one number by another

proper fraction a fraction with its numerator (top number) smaller than its denominator (bottom number) and so equal to less than 1

e.g. ⅞ but not ⁹⁄₈

Write out the sentences and fill in the missing words.

1   If "perpendicular" had been included in this dictionary, it would have come between _____ and _____. *(2 marks)*

2   In Miss Woolacott's class there are 30 children. Fifteen of them have brown hair. So _____ % of the class has brown hair. *(2 marks)*

3   Just two of these numbers are prime numbers: 5, 15, 17, 21, 84 and 100. The two prime numbers are ____ and ____. *(2 marks)*

4   Two examples of numbers in a pattern are given. The next number after 19 in the first example would be _____. *(1 mark)*

5   A pentagon has ____ sides. *(1 mark)*

6   The product of 4 and 2 is ___. *(1 mark)*

7   "Analysing" a pattern means _____. *(2 marks)*

8   "Maths" is an abbreviation of _____. *(2 marks)*

9   The opposite of "solid" is _____. *(2 marks)*

The angel of Nitshill Road

Scene 1: In the playground.

All-the-class: *(In a whisper chant)*
Here comes Barry Hunter,
Making people cry.
Who's he picking on today?
Poor old Penny!

Barry: Here I come. I'm a jet-fighter. Vroom-vroom.
Out of my way, everyone. Oh, no! It's Penny,
the Moving Mountain. She's too big to miss.
I'm going to crash!

Penny: Go away, Barry. Leave me alone.

Barry: Moving Mountain!

All-the-class: *(Whispering)* Penny's crying now.

Barry: I'm off. Vroom-vroom!

All-the-class: *(In a whisper chant)*
There goes Barry Hunter,
Making people cry.
Who's he picking on today?
Poor old Mark.

Barry: Where am I? I must have flown to Mars by mistake.
Here's Mark the Martian. He's got strange sticky-up
hair and glasses as thick as bottle ends. He can't be
human.

Mark: Push off, Barry Hunter.

Barry: He speaks! He can't catch a ball or save a goal, but
he can speak!

67

Mark:	Go away. Leave me alone.
Barry:	Watch me poke the Martian. Look, he's getting mad. He's glaring through his bionic eyes. He's getting his controls in order. He's crashing his gears. He's getting ready to hit me! *(Mark lashes out.)* He missed!
	(Barry runs off.)
All-the-class:	*(Whispering)* Look, Mark's crying now.
Lisa:	They ought to tell.
All-the-class:	Tell who?
Lisa:	Penny's big sister.
All-the-class:	Guess what she'd say. *(Imitating a big sister)* "Just stay away from him. Then he won't bother you."
Lisa:	That won't work, then. How about Mark's big brother?
All-the-class:	Guess what he'd say. *(Imitating a big brother)* "If he hits you, just you hit him back!"
Lisa:	That isn't going to work. We could tell the caretaker or the dinner lady.
All-the-class:	Guess what they'd say. *(Imitating)* "You'll all have to learn to sort yourselves out."
Lisa:	Well, that won't work. What about telling Mr Fairway?
All-the-class:	Guess what he'll say. *(Imitating Mr Fairway)* "Really, Mark, you bring a lot of it on yourself."
Lisa:	We'll have to tell their mothers, then.

68

All-the-class:	Guess what they'll say. *(Imitating)* "I'm going up the school if it doesn't stop."
Mark & Penny:	It hasn't stopped.
Lisa:	But they haven't gone.
All-the-class:	Stuck!
Lisa:	Watch out! The gate's opening. Barry must be coming back.

Anne Fine from *The Angel of Nitshill Road* (Ginn & Company)

 Answer in complete sentences.

1 How do we know that Barry Hunter has bullied people before? *(1 mark)*

2 Why do the rest of the class whisper when Barry is around? *(1 mark)*

3 Why does the nickname "Moving Mountain" hurt Penny so much? *(2 marks)*

4 Mark has poor eyesight. Mention two of Barry's cruel remarks about this. *(2 marks)*

5 If Penny's big sister advised her to keep out of Barry Hunter's way, what do you think Penny's answer would be? *(2 marks)*

6 Mark's big brother would probably tell him that Barry wouldn't bully him if he stood up for himself. Do you think he is right in this case? *(2 marks)*

7 Which two adults mentioned here probably think that children should sort out these problems by themselves? *(2 marks)*

8 One adult mentioned here would probably tell Mark that it was his own fault that he was bullied. What is his name? *(1 mark)*

9 If you were there, what would your advice be? *(2 marks)*

UNIT 33

Computer health

If you don't take care, you can damage your health working on computers – especially if you spend long stretches at the screen. But if you follow some simple guidelines, you can enjoy a danger-free time.

Eyes

Most monitors have an anti-glare screen. But if yours doesn't, wear tinted glasses. You may feel a bit silly wearing sunglasses indoors, but it could stop you getting headaches.

Eyes can become strained by focusing at the same distance for a long time. So, every ten minutes or so, look away from the screen and focus on something further away.

Posture

Sitting at a computer can strain your shoulders and the bottom of your back. So it is important to sit in a good chair. Find one that can be adjusted to support your lower back and allows you to have both feet on the floor. Your elbows and knees should be bent at 90°. Sit directly in front of your monitor and keyboard. Your keyboard should be at the same height as your elbows.

Shrug your shoulders and shake your hands regularly to relieve tension, which builds up in your muscles and joints.

RSS

Doctors think that an illness called **repetitive strain syndrome (RSS)** can be caused by working at a keyboard and using a mouse every day. It mostly affects wrists, fingers and arms, and has symptoms similar to arthritis. It can be very painful and forces people to give up work. When typing, make sure your wrists are completely relaxed and flat, never bent.

Taking breaks

Remember to take a 10-minute break every hour you work.
This will rest your eyes and other parts of your body.

Margaret Stephens and Rebecca Treays from *Computers for Beginners*
(Usborne Computer Guides)

 Write out the sentence from each pair that is true.
*(2 marks for every correct answer – plus 1 bonus mark for
attempting every question whether you get it right or not!)*

1   a) It is always advisable to wear sunglasses when working on a
     computer.
     b) It is sometimes advisable to wear sunglasses when working on a
     computer.

2   a) You should rest your eyes by looking away from the screen when
     they feel tired.
     b) You should rest your eyes by looking away from the screen every
     ten minutes or so.

3   a) When you are sitting at a keyboard, always make sure that your
     elbows are above the keyboard.
     b) When you are sitting at a keyboard, always make sure that your
     elbows are level with the keyboard.

4   a) Shrugging your shoulders can help to reduce the strain in your back.
     b) Shrugging your shoulders adds to the strain in your back.

5   a) Bending your wrists above the keys on a keyboard is the safest way
     of typing.
     b) Keeping your wrists flat as you type is the safest way of typing.

6   a) Using a mouse every day causes repetitive strain syndrome.
     b) Using a mouse every day can cause repetitive strain syndrome.

7   a) It is not possible to use computers safely.
     b) It is possible to use computers safely.

UNIT 34

Poetry in different forms

Church Choir *(haiku)*

The sopranos soar
Altos, bass and baritones
Keep feet on the ground

A Cello *(shape)*

My cello big and fat

makes

the sound

of a   screeching

rat. It   plays   F

double   sharp

when   I   want

it   to   play

B   flat.   It

sounds   like

a   bad   com-

position   when

I   play   in   the   4th

position.   If   I   try

to   play   vibrato   my

bow   goes all

s-t-a-c-c-

ato

!

Richard Lester from *O, Frabjous Day*
ed. Sandy Brownjohn (Ginn & Company)

There was a young lady (*limerick*)

There was a young lady from Bute
Who delighted in playing the flute.
She fingered and blew
And each note was true
That clever young lady from Bute.

Answer in complete sentences.

1   Look again at the haiku. How many syllables are there in it altogether?
    (1 mark)

2   Complete this sentence and write it out.
    **Line 1 of a haiku has ___ syllables, line 2 has ___ syllables and line 3
    has___ syllables.** *(3 marks)*

3   In what sense do the sopranos in the haiku "soar"? *(1 mark)*

4   In what sense do the rest of the choir keep their "feet on the ground"?
    (1 mark)

5   A limerick has five lines. Which lines rhyme with each other?
    (2 marks)

6   Write out the shape poem, "A Cello", as an 8-line poem.
    (3 marks)

7   Which do you like best, the 8-line version or the one in the shape of a
    cello? Give at least two reasons for your verdict. *(2 marks)*

8   Use your dictionary to find the meaning of these two words in "A
    Cello":
    a) **vibrato**
    b) **staccato** *(2 marks)*

Dear Householder

Barsetshire County Council
The Mall
Barset BS1 8EX

Dear Householder

Blue Bins Initiative

In line with the recycling initiative recently approved by the County Council, we shall be delivering, in the coming weeks, a blue wheelie bin to each household. This is in addition to the green bin you already have.

The blue bin is to be used for clean, dry waste that can be recycled. The green bin is for waste which must go to landfill sites.

From the beginning of October, your blue bins and green bins will be emptied on alternate weeks. Nearer the date, a calendar will be delivered to each household, so that you will know which bin to leave by the roadside on each collection day.

The following items can be recycled and should be placed in the blue bin:

- newspapers
- paper and envelopes
- plastic bottles and cartons, food tins and Tetra packs (washed, dried and crushed)
- shredded paper
- cardboard

Please <u>do not</u> place glass, tinfoil, or plastic bags and wrappings in the blue bin.

Glass jars and bottles should be brought to any official "Bottle Bank", of which there are many now sited at convenient locations around the County.

For those willing to compost garden and kitchen waste, we take this opportunity of reminding you that composters continue to be available at the subsidised cost of £25 from the Council. Full instructions will be provided.

Barsetshire County Council is proud of these environmental initiatives and invites your cooperation.

Yours sincerely

Samantha Drake

Samantha Drake, Environmental Awareness Officer

1   The blue bins have not yet been delivered to householders.

2   The blue bins will be emptied every week.

3   Damp paper should not be put in the blue bins.

4   Bottle Banks will be delivered to everyone before October.

5   The blue bins cost £25.

6   Plastic carrier bags should not be put in the blue bins, but plastic bottles can be.

7   Potato peelings and grass cuttings can be used to make compost.

8   Everybody must start to use a composter after October 1st.

9   Recycling means changing waste products into something that can be used again.

10 Jars and glass bottles can be recycled, but they should not be put in the blue bin.

11 The Council is proud that less waste will have to be buried in landfill sites.

UNIT 36
Drought

Sun hot
Hasn't rained
No water
Walked miles
But water's mud
River's dry
Can't bathe
Can't drink
Brown grass
No grass
Skeletons stare
From cracked earth

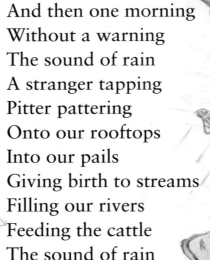

And then one morning
Without a warning
The sound of rain
A stranger tapping
Pitter pattering
Onto our rooftops
Into our pails
Giving birth to streams
Filling our rivers
Feeding the cattle
The sound of rain

We're all smiling
My father is hugging my
Mother
Children running naked
Mouths open towards the Gods
We're all laughing
Me forgetting to hide
The gap between my teeth.

Accabre Huntley from *Chasing the Sun* ed.
Sally Bacon (Simon and Schuster Young Books)

Answer in complete sentences.

1   Why do you think the writer has "walked miles"? *(2 marks)*

2   Why are the lines describing the drought very short and jerky? *(2 marks)*

3   a) Which three words are used to describe the sound of the rain on the rooftops? *(1 mark)*
b) Which two letters in these words make the same sound as the raindrops? *(1 mark)*

4   What is another word for "pails"? *(1 mark)*

5   a) Which line in the second verse is repeated? *(1 mark)*
b) If you were reading this poem to the class, how would you say this line? *(1 mark)*

6   The family are very happy now that it has started to rain after the long drought. Mention three things that they don't have to worry about now. *(3 marks)*

7   a) What clue are we given that the poet may be describing a childhood memory? *(1 mark)*
b) If it is a childhood memory, why has the poet chosen to write about it in the present tense? *(2 marks)*

Evacuation

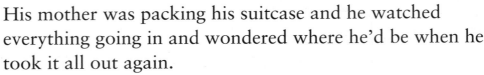

His mother was packing his suitcase and he watched everything going in and wondered where he'd be when he took it all out again.

"They said only one case, so there's only room for one change of clothes. All the things you wanted, they're at the bottom. I'll send on the rest as soon as I know where you'll be." She smoothed down his coat collar and brushed through his hair with her fingers. "You'll do," she said, smiling softly.

"Do I have to, Mum? Do I have to go?" Even as he asked he knew it was useless. Everyone was going from school – no one was staying behind. He was ashamed of himself now. He'd promised himself he'd be brave when he said goodbye. He clung to his mother, pressing his face into her coat, fighting his tears.

She crouched down in front of him, holding him by the shoulders. "You remember what I said, David, when I told you your father had been killed? Do you?" David nodded. "I said you'd have to be the man in the house, remember?" He took the handkerchief she was offering. "You never saw your father crying, did you?"

"No, Mum."

"Men don't cry, see? Try to be a man, David, like your father was, eh?" She chucked him under the chin, and straightened his cap. "Come on now. We'll be late."

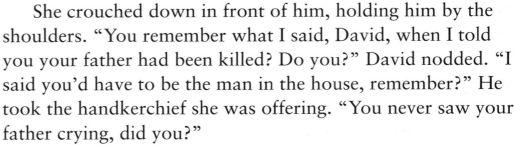

It was still dark up in the street, and a fine drizzle sprayed their faces as they walked away from the house. David looked back as they came to the postbox at the corner and caught a last glimpse of the front steps. He felt his mother's hand on his elbow, and then they were round the corner.

Ahead of them there was a glow of fire in the sky. "South of the river," his mother said. "Battersea, I should say. Poor

devils. At least you'll be away from all that, David, away from
the bombs, away from the war. At least they won't get you as
well." He was surprised by the grim tone in her voice.

"Where will you go, Mum?"

"Wherever they send me. Probably to the coast – Kent or
somewhere like that. Somewhere where there's anti-aircraft
guns, that's all I know. Don't worry. I'll write.

Their footsteps sounded hollow in the empty street. They
had to step off the pavement to pick their way round a pile of
rubble that was still scattered halfway across the street. That
was where the Perkins family had lived. They had been bombed
out only a week before; they were all killed. Special prayers were
said at assembly for Brian and Garry Perkins, but no one ever
mentioned them after that. They were dead, after all.

In the gloom outside Highbury and Islington Underground
Station there was already a crowd of people. Miss Evers' voice
rang out above the hubbub and the crying. She was calling out
names. His mother pulled him and they ran the last few yards.

"Tony Tucker. Tony Tucker." Miss Evers' voice rose to a
shriek. "Where's Tucky? Has anyone seen Tucky?"

"He's coming, miss. I saw him."

"And what about David Carey? Is he here yet?"

"Yes, miss. I'm here, miss." David spoke out, pleased at the
strength in his voice.

"Here's Tucky, miss. He's just coming."

"Right then." Miss Evers folded her piece of paper. "We're
all here, and it's time to go. Say goodbye as quick as ever you
can. The train leaves Paddington at half past eight, and we have
to be there at least an hour before. So hurry it up now – and
don't forget your gas masks."

David felt the case being handed to him. "Goodbye, David.
And don't worry. It'll be all right. I'll send a letter as soon as I
can. God bless." She kissed him quickly on the cheek and turned

away. He watched her until she disappeared at the end of the street. All around him there was crying: boys he'd never dreamt could cry, weeping openly, and mothers holding on to each other as they walked away. He was glad his mother hadn't cried, and it helped him to see so many of his friends as miserable as he felt himself. He blinked back the tears that had gathered in his eyes and wiped his face before turning towards the station.

Michael Morpugo from *Friend or Foe* (Mammoth)

 Answer in complete sentences.

1 What special reason does David have for trying to be brave? *(2 marks)*

2 What may have happened in Battersea to cause the "glow of fire"? *(1 mark)*

3 How did Brian Perkins die? *(1 mark)*

4 Why is David's school being evacuated to the country? *(2 marks)*

5 How many pupils in David's class are staying behind in London? *(1 mark)*

6 Which one of these adjectives best describes how David's mother feels about his going away? Why?
angry   amused   relieved   impatient *(2 marks)*

7 What is Tony Tucker's nickname? *(1 mark)*

8 How does David feel about leaving London and his mother? *(1 mark)*

9 David has two items of luggage. What are they? *(2 marks)*

10 Explain the meaning of the underlined words:
She <u>chucked</u> him under the chin.
Miss Evers' voice rang out <u>above the hubbub</u>. *(2 marks)*